65930032R00062

Made in the USA
Middletown, DE
06 March 2018